CARNIVORES

By Harriet Brundle

BookLife
PUBLISHING

©2019
**BookLife Publishing
King's Lynn
Norfolk PE30 4LS**

All rights reserved.
Printed in Malaysia.

A catalogue record for this
book is available from the
British Library.

ISBN: 978-1-78637-464-6

Written by:
Harriet Brundle

Edited by:
Holly Duhig

Designed by:
Jasmine Pointer

Photocredits:
Images are courtesy of Shutterstock.com. With thanks to Getty Images, Thinkstock Photo and iStockphoto.
Front cover - ehtesham, Anna Kucherova, Songsak P, reptiles4all, Eric Isselee, willmetts, MaraZe, Kuttelvaserova Stuchelova. 2- PhotocechCZ.
3 - reptiles4all. 4 - Jan Stria. 5 - Paul Broadbent. 6 - Irina Kozorog. 7 - Ewa Studio. 8 - wildestanimal. 9 - Oleg Blazhyievskyi. 10 - Ondrej Prosicky,
Santiparp Wattanaporn. 11 - Utekhina Anna. 12 - Utopia_88. 13 - gualtiero boffi. 14 - 249 Anurak. 15 - Bokeh Blur Background. 16 - Camilo Torres.
17 - Alex Coan, Christian Musat, Four Oaks, Kotomiti Okuma, JIANG HONGYAN, Nosyrevy, VanderWolf Images, Oleksandr Lytvynenko, D_M, Eric
Isselee, Pakhnyushchy, Le Do, PetlinDmitry, NERYXCOM, Aaron Ama, Choksawatdikorn, LeonP, Tono Balaguer. 18 - Satirus. 19 - Gerald Mark Griffin.
20 - Phil Stev. 21 - Shaiith. 22 - Patila. 23 - JonathanC Photography, Nenad Nedomacki.

CONTENTS

Words that look like this can be found in the glossary on page 24.

ALL ABOUT FOOD

Animals need food, water, air, and shelter in order to stay alive. Food is very important because it is full of <u>nutrients</u> that provide the energy animals need to move and grow.

Animals also need energy to do important jobs such as breathing and <u>digesting</u> their food.

This spider is waiting for its dinner to land on its web.

You are a living thing and so you need food to survive too. Food for animals comes in lots of different shapes and sizes. You might enjoy a bowl of pasta for your dinner while a spider might prefer a fly or two for theirs!

WHAT IS A CARNIVORE?

A carnivore is an <u>organism</u> that eats meat. Carnivores eat other animals to get the nutrients they need. For example, hawks eat mice and African wild dogs eat wildebeest.

Some types of carnivores eat mainly fish, while others eat insects.

Cows are herbivores.

Some carnivores use lots of energy and must feed very often. Others use less energy and can go longer between their meals.

Carnivores might eat other carnivorous animals or they might feed on herbivores or omnivores too. Herbivores are animals that only eat plant matter while omnivores eat both meat and plants.

PREDATORS

Predators are carnivorous animals that must find, catch and kill other animals for the food they need to survive. Predators come in a range of different shapes and sizes. A huge crocodile and a tiny weasel are both predators!

Under the sea there are lots of different predators, such as the great white shark.

Some snakes bite their prey. Other snakes will wrap themselves around the animal <u>extremely</u> tightly.

Predators have <u>adaptations</u> which help them to catch their food. Some animals work in groups, or use <u>camouflage</u> to sneak up on their prey. Other predators try to outrun the animal they want to catch.

PREY

Prey is any animal which is hunted and caught by a predator. Predators need prey to survive. An animal can be a predator and prey at the same time.

A seal is prey when it is hunted by a polar bear but the seal becomes the predator when it catches fish to eat.

This hedgehog has spikes to protect itself from predators such as foxes.

Prey have adaptations too. These adaptations help them to avoid being caught by predators. Some prey live together in large groups for <u>protection</u>. Other prey might use camouflage, spikes, spines, shells or stings to protect themselves.

SCAVENGERS

Scavengers are animals that feed on the meat of animals which have been killed by another predator or have died <u>naturally</u>. After the predators have finished eating, there are usually scraps of meat or bone left behind that scavengers eat.

Vultures are scavengers.

Hyenas have very strong jaws which they use to crush up bones.

Hyenas are scavengers. Although a pack of hyenas will hunt for their food, they will also make the most of what has been left behind by other animals when given the chance.

THE FOOD CHAIN

A food chain shows the different organisms that rely on each other for the food they need. Food chains start with a producer, which is something that makes its own food, such as a plant.

Plants make their food through a process called photosynthesis.

Some animals are found in more than one food chain.

After the producers, the other organisms in the food chain are known as consumers. Most food chains will include an omnivore or herbivore which eats the plants and a carnivore which eats other animals.

Lots of food chains that link together are known as a food web.

Each of the arrows in a food chain points to the predator. These arrows show the way the energy is moving. As the animal eats its prey, the prey becomes energy for the predator.

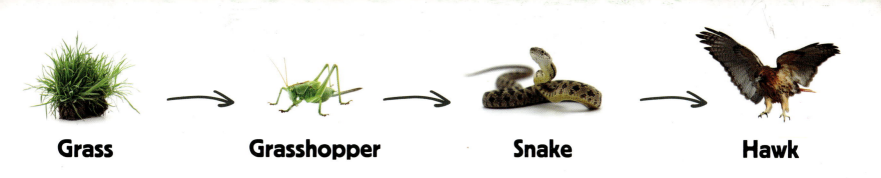

Grass → **Grasshopper** → **Snake** → **Hawk**

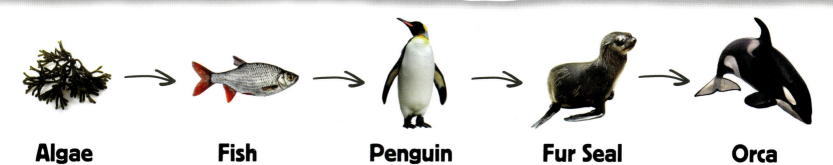

Algae → **Fish** → **Penguin** → **Fur Seal** → **Orca**

Grain → **Mouse** → **Fox** → **Lynx**

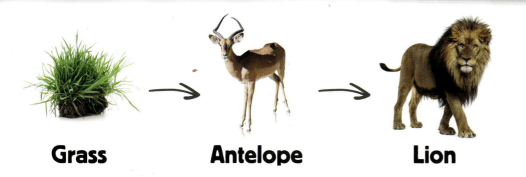

Grass → **Antelope** → **Lion**

Carnivores at the top of the food chain are called apex predators.

Algae → **Zooplankton** → **Fish** → **Reef Shark**

TEETH AND JAWS

Carnivores have sharp incisors and pointed canine teeth. These are used to kill and eat their prey. Carnivores need sharp teeth to tear up their food.

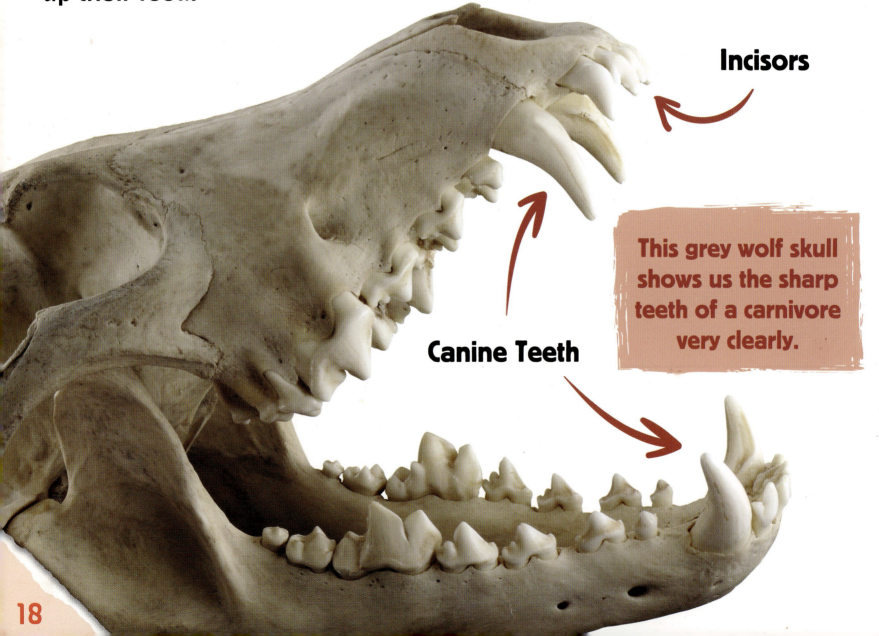

Incisors

Canine Teeth

This grey wolf skull shows us the sharp teeth of a carnivore very clearly.

The Nile crocodile has the strongest bite of any animal.

Usually, carnivores can only open and close their jaws up and down. This gives them a very strong, snapping bite. They can't move their jaws from side to side, so can't grind vegetables at all.

DIGESTION

Different animals have different digestive systems that are better suited to dealing with the types of food they eat. Unlike some other animals, carnivores usually have only one stomach which is suited to digesting meat.

Most carnivore digestive systems are unable to digest any plant material at all.

The size of a carnivore's stomach is usually large enough for it to eat bigger meals in one go, rather than having to graze. Carnivores often have to work hard for their dinner, so their bodies are adapted so that they don't have to do it so often!

CREATIVE CARNIVORES

Although most carnivores are animals, some plants are carnivores too! The Venus fly trap catches insects in its spiky leaves.

Venus Fly Trap

One of the world's biggest animals, the blue whale, is a carnivore. It filters huge amounts of water with its mouth and eats <u>krill</u>.

Spiders use webs to catch their prey. A spider will spin its web and then lay in wait for an animal such as a fly to become trapped in the sticky threads.

Cheetah

One of the world's fastest animals, the cheetah, is a carnivore. Cheetahs creep up to their prey and then use their speed to catch it.

GLOSSARY

adaptations	when something changes to be better suited to its environment
camouflage	a way of hiding
digesting	the process of food being broken down in the body
grazing	eating grass and other plants slowly throughout the day
krill	a small animal with a shell which lives in the sea
naturally	as a result of nature
nutrients	needed for life and growth
organism	a type of life form such as an animal
photosynthesis	when plants use energy from light to make their own food
protection	being made safe from injury or harm

INDEX